This book belongs to:

Simply Christmas

A BUSY MOM'S GUIDE TO RECLAIMING THE PEACE OF THE HOLIDAYS

TAMA FORTNER

Ink &
Willow

Dear Mama,

I'VE BEEN THERE. I know what you're up against. The pressure to create the perfect Christmas celebration for those we love. To bake the perfect cookies, host the perfect party, find the perfect gifts. And then there are trees to decorate, stockings to hang, parties to plan, cards to create, and, and, and . . .

We rush and scurry from one event and obligation to the next, until all-too-soon, it's December 26, and we're staring at a pile of empty boxes and crumpled wrapping paper, wondering how we missed the joy.

It doesn't have to be that way.

This book isn't going to give you any quick-fix, one-size-fits-all answers. Nor do I have the ultimate checklist that will solve all your problems in a blinding whirlwind of organization. What I do have are some thoughts about that long-ago first Christmas, along with a few practical tips for simplifying the season and staying mindful of the true reasons we celebrate it.

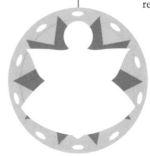

To use this book, simply read one devotion each day. These thirty-one devotions are not dated, so you're welcome to begin reading on December 1, December 15, the day after Thanksgiving, or the middle of July—without even a smidgen of guilt or shame. Pray the prayer, meditate on the "Remember" thought and try out the "Reclaiming Christmas" tip—if you want to. No pressure. Use the tips that work for you, and simply skip the rest. Seriously. Just skip 'em. And if you miss a day, don't worry. After all, Christ isn't just for Christmas, and He's worth celebrating every day of the year.

Simply Christmas is your invitation to slow down and savor this time with the Savior. And it's your permission to kick the pressures of perfection to the curb.

This year, let's choose to pause and to ponder as Mary did, to get lost in the wonder of Immanuel, of God with us. This year, let it be simply Christmas.

—Tama

DAY

1

**The Light
–of–
Christmas**

The Word gave life to everything
that was created, and his life
brought light to everyone.

JOHN 1:4, NLT

The Christmas season is filled with lights—on the trees, on our homes, and in the eyes of little ones glittering with excitement. Even the Christmas story itself is filled with light. The heaven-bright angels that lit up the shepherds' dark skies, the shining star that the wise men followed, and most radiant of all, the light of God's own Son born into the world and so gently laid in that Bethlehem manger.

That light still shines.

But do we see it? Or have we allowed it to be dimmed by the endless onslaught of tasks and to-dos?

Maybe the questions you're asking right now are, *How do I see that light? How can I get it to shine in my life and chase away the darkness?* Because you—like me, like each and every one of us courageous enough, or perhaps desperate enough, to admit it—need that light. How do we find it?

In a world where so few answers are simple, this one is: *the Word.* It is the good news Jesus came to give. It is the light to guide our path and chase away the darkness.

*Mighty God, Wonderful Counselor, guide me—
this day and every day—by the light
of Your holy Word. Amen.*

Remember

Open up the Light
of Christmas and
let it shine.

RECLAIMING CHRISTMAS

Take a moment to ponder what you really want out of this Christmas season. What is most important to you? What feelings and experiences do you want to be sure are included, both for yourself and your family? And what would you rather live without? Be honest—no one else has to see this list! Let these answers help guide your yeses and nos as you seek His Light in the coming days of celebration and chaos.

*Highly
Favored*

The angel went to her and said,
"Greetings, you who are highly
favored! The Lord is with you."

LUKE 1:28

To the world, Mary was just a poor girl from a poor village. Young, insignificant, and unimportant. So when the angel appeared and declared her to be "highly favored," I suspect Mary didn't feel that way at all. In fact, the very next verse tells us that she was "startled" (NCV), "confused" (NLT), and even "greatly troubled" (NIV) by the angel's greeting.

We don't have to dig too deep to understand why, do we? Because though many things have changed between Mary's time and ours, one thing has not—our simultaneous longing and reluctance to feel *highly favored*. With all its subtle and not-so-subtle competitions and comparisons, Christmas sometimes seems to highlight all our self-perceived shortcomings. It's so easy to look around at others and feel insignificant, unimportant.

Don't listen to the doubts. We are—you are, I am—highly favored.

If those words startle, confuse, or trouble, let the angel's answer to Mary's fears be the answer to our own: "Don't be afraid . . . God has shown you his grace" (Luke 1:30, NCV). The "free, spontaneous, absolute favor and loving-kindness" (AMPC) of God's grace is *ours*. Not because of what we do or don't do, but simply because of who we are: *His*. We don't need an angel to tell us that. God Himself has told us. The message is there in the manger. We—you and I—are highly favored because the Lord has chosen to be with us.

Lord of lords, teach my heart to believe that
I am highly favored by You. Amen.

Remember

Grace is the
message of
the manger.

RECLAIMING CHRISTMAS

A children's librarian once told our group of young moms gathered in her story hour—with toddlers in our laps, around our necks, and on our backs—that slice-and-bake cookies don't count. And I believed her. For *years*. Why? Because I was trying to live up to everyone else's expectations of who I should be. Because I wanted to be highly favored. I now know the truth: *slice-and-bake cookies count*. So do break-aparts, no-bakes, and made from scratch, roll out, and frost cookies. It's not about the cookies. It's about time spent together.

*Bonus Tip: Sprinkle those slices of sugar cookie dough with cinnamon and sugar for super-easy, super-yummy snickerdoodles.

Servant
–of–
Servants

"I am the Lord's servant."

LUKE 1:38

Can I be honest? *Servant* is not my favorite word. That's because there are days when I feel it describes a bit too much of my life, particularly around the holidays. And to be brutally honest, there are times when I feel completely "served out." Can you relate?

Perhaps that's why I stumble over this one line of Mary's reply: "I am the Lord's servant." Yes, I know she's talking to an angel. But that word, *servant*, still gives me pause.

Yet Mary offered it without hesitation. As a woman of that time (and a poor woman, at that), she surely knew what it was to serve. If something needed doing, it was likely Mary's hands that would be found doing it. Or a mother's, sister's, or cousin's.

Then I remember that her answer wasn't really for the angel; it was for the Lord. The One who sent His Son to Mary's womb, to the manger in Bethlehem, to the Garden of Gethsemane. And that Son, the Servant of servants, came to seek, save, and serve us.

Could it be that *servant* is something far less Cinderella and something far more lovely? For in serving those made in His image, we both mirror and serve the King. So when the next chore on that endless list of must-be-dones beckons, remember the words of the One who was born to serve: "Truly I tell you, whatever you did for one of the least of these . . . you did for me" (Matthew 25:40).

O Holy Lord, when I am tired and frustrated
and feeling "served out," remind me of all that
Jesus did to serve and to save me. Amen.

Remember

In serving, we
both mirror and
serve the King.

RECLAIMING CHRISTMAS

When the Christmas chaos starts to get the best of you, take
a night off from the kitchen and the entertaining of littles and
bigs. Corral everyone into the TV room, set up your favorite
Christmas movie, and serve up a pizza picnic on the floor. Skip
the plates and enjoy the slices right out of the box. Finish off
the night with popcorn and snuggles. No, it isn't an escape to a
tropical isle, but there's no cooking, and cleanup is a breeze!

DAY

4

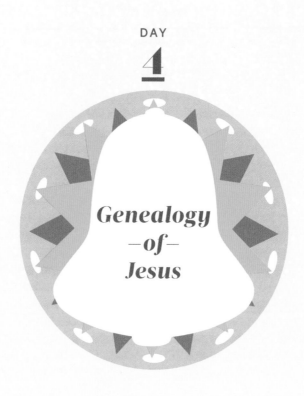

Genealogy
—of—
Jesus

This is the genealogy of Jesus
the Messiah the son of David.

MATTHEW 1:1

Tucked away in the genealogy of Jesus, amid all that testosterone, are a few feminine names. First up, there's Rahab, who entertained more than her fair share of friends. Next, you'll find Tamar, who in desperate times resorted to desperate measures. Ruth, a foreigner, grew up on the wrong side of the Dead Sea. And Uriah's wife—better known as Bathsheba—well, we've all heard the stories about her and King David.

I love these ladies. Each and every one. They don't exactly exemplify the perfection of Proverbs 31, but that's why they make my heart smile. Because with all their faults, missteps, and mistakes, God made a place for them in the genealogy of Jesus. That means there's also a place for me—in spite of all my own faults, missteps, and mistakes, which so often seem to be spotlighted around this time of year. I picture these ladies, as part of that "great cloud of witnesses" (Hebrews 12:1), oohing and aahing over the little One in the manger. There's a place for them there.

And guess what? There's a place for you and for me too.

Our names might not be inscribed in the pages of the Word, but as daughters of the King, our names are inscribed on the palms of His hands, in the Book of Life, and, yes, in the genealogy of Jesus.

Lord God Almighty, You are perfect in all Your ways, and I am so not perfect. Yet You still welcome me into Your family. And for that I praise You. Amen.

Remember

You are a daughter of the King, and God has a place for you.

RECLAIMING CHRISTMAS

For years, my husband and I (okay, mostly my husband) would drag out the Christmas lights to decorate all the trees and bushes around the house. Honestly, it wasn't fun. It just felt like something we *should* do. We pushed ourselves to get it "perfect," and it just never was. Let me suggest an alternative: go see *other people's* lights. (Many cities offer self-guided tours of the best displays.) Pick a night, dress everyone in their Christmas cozies, and pile into the car. Load up with spill-proof cups of hot chocolate, baggies of marshmallows, and a cookie or two. Then *ooh* and *aah* over all those beautiful Christmas lights sparkling in the darkness. Lights that you didn't have to put up and you don't have to take down.

*Christmas
Competition*

Elizabeth gave a glad cry and exclaimed
to Mary, "God has blessed you above all
women, and your child is blessed."

LUKE 1:42, NLT

Elizabeth often gets tossed into the background of the Christmas story. We remember her as the one whose babe leapt in her womb when Mary entered the room. But Elizabeth must have been such a special person. After all, it was she that Mary first ran to with the news that she would be the mother of the Son of God.

And remember, when Mary rushed in that day, Elizabeth was in the midst of her own miracle—pregnant after so many years of waiting. How easy it would have been for her to be jealous or even a bit angry with Mary for eclipsing her own special time. But Elizabeth was neither angry nor jealous. Instead, she was both thrilled for Mary and filled with praise for the God they both loved.

The holidays can be a time when differences are magnified, whether it's in income, gifts, or talents and abilities. I confess, my eyes sometimes become fixated on what others have and are able to do. In comparison, I feel . . . *lacking*. Which is so utterly and completely foolish. Christmas isn't a competition. I—you, we—have been given the richest gift of all: a Savior! Let's fix our eyes on Him.

Lord, help me keep my eyes fixed on
You, the greatest of all gifts. Amen.

RECLAIMING CHRISTMAS

My friend builds the most incredibly elaborate gingerbread house. With her kids. *Every* Christmas. It's a homemade, two-storied, sugar-coated, confectionary dream decorated with every kind of candy found on aisle 4 of the grocery store. I build a gingerbread house too. With my kids. Every Christmas (okay, *almost* every Christmas). It's from a kit we buy at the craft store that's roughly the size of a tissue box. And do you know what? It's perfect for us. Don't compete. Do what works for you.

*Bonus Tip: If you're not planning on eating your gingerbread house, skip the sugar-glue that comes in those kits and just hot glue that house together. Trust me. You'll thank me later.

Believe
–and–
Be Blessed

Blessed is she who has
believed that the Lord would
fulfill his promises to her!

LUKE 1:45

Mary believed.

She listened to the angel's astonishing words, and she believed it was not only possible for the Lord to do all He had promised, but that He would actually do it.

Because Mary believed the promises of God, she–and we–are blessed.

Believe. Could it really be that simple? For all those promises God has made to you, to me, to each of us, is believing the key to claiming their power in our lives? *Yes!*

When you're feeling worn out and unworthy, when there's too much to do and too little of you, when the spilled milk really does seem like a reason to cry . . . believe!

Believe God is with you, lending you His strength and covering you with His grace. Believe He will fill you with His peace and joy. And believe in the greatest promise of all–that you are incomprehensibly loved by the God of all creation. His love is so deep, so rich, so high and wide, that He sent His only Son to a dusty manger and to a rugged cross.

Simply believe, and you will be blessed.

Holy Father, I do believe.
And when it is hard, help me to
believe anyway. Amen.

Remember

Believing opens
the door to the
blessings of God.

RECLAIMING CHRISTMAS

My husband and I are blessed with a generous family. But after those first couple of Christmases with kiddos, we were drowning in that generosity. So. Many. Toys. And I get it. A grandparent's greatest fun is in seeing a little one's eyes light up when a hoped-for toy is finally in hand. But again . . . *so many toys*. So we negotiated a compromise. Grandparents buy something from a "wish" list and something from a "need" list—and maybe a couple of other little things. (After all, spoiling and grandparents go hand-in-hand.) Then the rest of their Christmas "budget" goes into a school and college fund. A blessing for now and a blessing for later. And not *quite* so many toys.

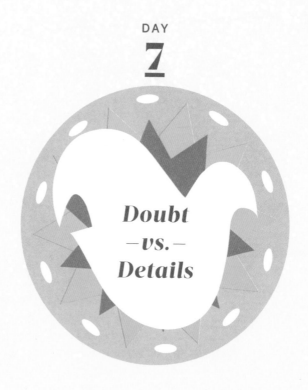

Doubt
—vs.—
Details

Zechariah said to the angel,
"How can I know that what you say is true?"
. . . Mary said to the angel,
"How will this happen?"

LUKE 1:18, 34, NCV

It might appear that Zechariah and Mary ask very similar questions of the angel in Luke 1. But look closer, and you'll see that they are quite different. While Zechariah voices doubt, Mary is simply seeking details.

The answer to both questions is the same: God.

With God, nothing is impossible. He is both stronger than any doubt and able to cover all the details.

This holiday season, we will face the seemingly impossible—and I don't just mean that never-ending to-do list. We'll be asked to love the unlovable, to keep the peace with those bent on destroying it, to hold our tongues when we'd dearly love to let them loose, and to give when we feel we've nothing left to give. Most important, we'll be challenged to shine the light of Jesus into the hearts and celebrations of our children, our family, our friends, and all who cross our paths.

When the impossibility of it all overwhelms, when doubts arise, and when the details of how and when and where threaten to drown, remember the answer to it all: God. Our doubts do not diminish His power nor His desire to work in the details of our lives.

O Lord my God, shine Your light so brightly
into my life that it conquers all doubts
and all worries about details. Amen.

Remember

Our doubts do not
diminish God's power
to work in the
details of our lives.

RECLAIMING CHRISTMAS

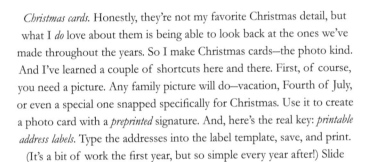

Christmas cards. Honestly, they're not my favorite Christmas detail, but what I *do* love about them is being able to look back at the ones we've made throughout the years. So I make Christmas cards—the photo kind. And I've learned a couple of shortcuts here and there. First, of course, you need a picture. Any family picture will do—vacation, Fourth of July, or even a special one snapped specifically for Christmas. Use it to create a photo card with a *preprinted* signature. And, here's the real key: *printable address labels.* Type the addresses into the label template, save, and print. (It's a bit of work the first year, but so simple every year after!) Slide cards into envelopes, add labels and stamps, seal, mail—and done!

DAY

8

Mindful
—of—
You

My spirit rejoices in God my Savior,
for he has been mindful of the
humble state of his servant.

LUKE 1:47—48

Of all the many wonders of God, there is one that never ceases to amaze me, never ceases to steal my breath away and make my soul sing, and it is this: the God of all creation—the God who flung the stars into the sky, who holds the oceans in His hand, who used the birth of a tiny Babe in Bethlehem to sound the death knell on sin and death—is mindful of me.

You. Me. Each of us.

Our Lord is *El Roi* . . . the God who sees me. The same God who saw Hagar lost in the desert and desperation, who saw the disgraced Samaritan slipping to the well in the heat of the day, and who saw the woman thrown down in the dirt of sin and chose to lift her to life with His grace.

The almighty, all-powerful, always loving God counts the stars in the sky, the hairs on your head, and the tears you try to hide.

And like Mary, with that sweet and certain knowledge tucked into your heart, your spirit can rejoice in God your Savior.

He is *El Roi*—the God who sees, knows, and adores you. And He is mindful of you.

El Roi, thank You
for being mindful of me.
Amen.

Remember

He is *El Roi*–the One
who sees every star
in the sky and every
detail of your life.

RECLAIMING CHRISTMAS

God is mindful of you, but do you remember to be mindful of
yourself? In the scramble of the season, capturing all those precious
moments on your camera is a mom's must. But don't forget to get
in the picture yourself now and then. Stop worrying about your
hair or clothes or those few extra pounds you were hoping to lose.
You are beautiful in the love you give, and your loved ones will want
photos to remember you and your love in the years to come. Step
out from behind the camera, and smile for a picture or two with your
kids. They—and your future self—will thank you for the memories.

Seeking
—and—
Finding

The Mighty One has done
great things for me.

LUKE 1:49

Mary's song in Luke 1 is filled with praises. She looks at her life—a life that God has told her is about to become nothing at all like she had once planned—and declares that "the Mighty One has done great things for me."

Sometimes in the crush of day-to-day life, it can feel as if we're barely surviving. A spill, a sudden fever, a changed deadline. Nothing goes according to our carefully constructed plans.

When you begin to feel overwhelmed, pause. Breathe. Seek out the great things the Mighty One has done for you. Look past the piled-up dishes, the bits of breakfast waiting to be swept away, the cleats scattering mud crumbs across the floor, and see the home, the people—big and small—who fill it. Breathe in the sweet—and yes, the not-so-sweet—scents of this life the Lord has blessed you with. The very one that so rarely goes exactly as you'd planned.

Seek and you shall find all the blessings God has poured into your life. Sticky fingers and sticky grins, laughter, and arms reaching up to hug and to hold. Seek and you shall find . . . God.

The Mighty One has indeed done great things for us.

Almighty Lord, open my eyes to see all the blessings You have poured into even the messiest moments of my life. Amen.

Remember

Seek out the blessings,
and you will
find God.

RECLAIMING CHRISTMAS

You don't want to go to the party, the outing, the dinner, the gathering, the *whatever,* but there are times when you just can't say no—short of the plague or a raging fever, and even then it's dicey. When I'm stuck where I don't want to be, I find that the old advice is still so true: stop thinking about myself—whether my outfit is right or just how long I have before my updo comes crashing down—and think of someone else instead. Join the one who's sitting alone, listen to that preteen caught squarely between shyness and anxiousness to be all grown up, lend a hand to that other mom who just needs a moment of peace. Seek to be a blessing, and you'll find yourself blessed, even when you're where you'd rather not be.

DAY

10

*Not Part
–of the–
Plan*

In those days Caesar Augustus issued a
decree that a census should be taken of
the entire Roman world. . . . And everyone
went to their own town to register.

LUKE 2:1–3

Life was already very different from the way Mary had expected it to be. As a young, soon-to-be-new mother she surely must have hoped to have her baby amid the familiar comforts of home. But a decree from a faraway Roman emperor changed that too. With no choice but to comply, she and Joseph departed for Bethlehem, destined for a stranger's stable.

It may not have been what Mary hoped for, but it was what the Lord had foretold (Micah 5:2). And so the Son of God came to be born in Bethlehem.

Sometimes—especially, it seems, around the holiday season—we find ourselves at the mercy of things beyond our control. Our plans are changed by sickness, by storm, by circumstances, and we have no choice but to comply. Instead of stressing over what was supposed to be, stop and consider what could be.

Is it possible that this disruption to our carefully laid plans is part of God's greater plan? Could He use this sickness, this storm, this circumstance to work in our lives, in the lives of our loved ones, for a much greater good?

After all, Bethlehem may not have been part of Mary's "before the angel came and changed everything" plan, but it was part of God's perfect plan.

O Lord, when my own plans are
changed, help me to trust in
Your perfect plan. Amen.

Remember

A change in plans just
might be part of
God's perfect plan.

RECLAIMING CHRISTMAS

For years, my children sprinkled raw oats mixed with a bit of glitter across the front lawn. It served both as shimmering landing lights and a tasty snack for Santa's reindeer. It was one of my favorite traditions. That is, until I realized it was no longer one of theirs. Traditions can be beautiful and the source of sweet memories. They can also strangle the joy out of celebrations if they've been outgrown, are accompanied by too many eye rolls, or become more stressful than rewarding. This year, take stock of your family's traditions. Which ones are loved and important? Which ones need a bit of renewing and refreshing? And which ones need to be kicked to the curb?

Give
Grace

It is by grace you have been saved,
through faith—and this is not from
yourselves, it is the gift of God—not by
works, so that no one can boast.

EPHESIANS 2:8–9

Let's just get this troublesome little truth out of the way right now. You're going to mess up. I'm going to mess up. We're going to mess up.

At some point in the season, we're going to lose our temper when we should have found our patience. We're going to do what we shouldn't do. And the very words we promised ourselves we wouldn't say are going to go slip-sliding right across our lips. Eyes filled with hurt or snapping with anger are going to be looking our way. Because we aren't perfect.

So what do you do? Apologize. Reset. Regroup. Do what you can to undo the damage you've done. And then . . . *grace*, Mama. Give yourself grace. Don't forget for a moment that's why that Baby was born in Bethlehem! To give you His grace.

Gather yourself, dust off the shame and embarrassment, and keep doing the best you can do. Because God doesn't ask you to be perfect. He simply asks you to be His.

God of Mercy, when I mess up–
and we both know I will–help me to
accept the grace You give me. Amen.

Remember

Grace is God's gift
of love to you.

RECLAIMING CHRISTMAS

There's always at least one person I forget to shop for. In my defense,
it's usually someone I wasn't expecting to receive a gift from.
I don't know about you, but few things are more awkward and icky
for me than accepting a gift with nothing to give in return. I've
learned my lesson, and I now keep a stash of gifts. They're simple
and somewhat generic so they can be easily recycled as emergency
birthday gifts later on. Simply tuck a gift card, a devotional book,
or a candle into a pretty bag with pretty tissue. Keep one in the car
and one in a closet. Deliver as needed with a smile and a hug.

The Journey

Because Joseph was a descendant of King David, he
had to go to Bethlehem in Judea, David's ancient
home. He traveled there from the village of Nazareth
in Galilee. He took with him Mary, to whom he
was engaged, who was now expecting a child.

LUKE 2:4–5, NLT

With Caesar's decree for all of the Roman Empire to be counted, Mary and Joseph were sent on a journey to Bethlehem.

Imagine . . . nine months pregnant and forced to hit the road. Scholars say it was a three-day trip at best, possibly longer for a woman with child. Tradition and all those beautiful Christmas cards tell us Mary traveled on a donkey. But because of their poverty, she may not have enjoyed such a luxury. Donkey or no, this was no easy journey. And while sleeping under the stars might *sound* lovely, the reality was likely less picturesque.

All along that bumpy, uneven road, Mary carried the Savior within her. And I don't believe I'm being too bold when I say that God, just as surely, carried Mary through the days and over the miles to the city where the Lord had declared His Son would be born.

The journey through the Christmas season often has miles for us to travel. Allow God to carry you—just as He carried Mary so long ago. Through the days, over the miles, and across the bumpy, uneven terrain to the manger where His Son was born.

Father, please carry me through the miles
and over the bumps of this holiday season,
and lead me to the joy of Your Son. Amen.

Remember

Allow God to carry you this Christmas season.

RECLAIMING CHRISTMAS

Thankfully our Christmas journeys usually involve much faster modes of transportation than a donkey, but traveling with children can still present a challenge. Make these trips less stressful and more pleasant with a little creativity and a quick trip to the dollar store. Load up on coloring books, crayons, tiny toys, snacks, and other inexpensive goodies. You can even wrap them, if you like. At intervals throughout the trip, pull a treat out of the bag. (Pack a couple for yourself too!) The excitement of something new takes the edge off an endless car ride—and gives parents a bit of peace on the journey.

Bonus Tip: It cuts down on screen time—and mama guilt!

*Making
Room*

And she brought forth her firstborn Son,
and wrapped Him in swaddling cloths,
and laid Him in a manger, because there
was no room for them in the inn.

LUKE 2:7, NKJV

In the Christmas story, the innkeeper definitely falls on the villains' side of the cast. Usually seen as a cold, unfeeling Scrooge, he shuts the door firmly against Joseph and Mary, as he calls out, "No room!" His sense of hospitality is surely and sorely lacking.

Hospitality. For some, it comes so easily. But I'll confess it's a struggle of mine at times. Whether it's nagging feelings of unmet expectations or my own insecurities and perfectionism, hosting has too often seemed too overwhelming and simply *too much*. And so, for a long time, I didn't. But now I do. Or, at least, I'm trying to.

The truth is, if you come to our home, you'll likely find dust on the shelves, laundry in assorted states of completion, and crumbs on the breakfast table. There, I've said it.

But, honestly, does any of that really matter? Because let me say this, too: if you come to our home, you'll also find room to kick off your shoes, curl up on the couch, and help yourself to whatever might be in the fridge. You'll find room for a welcoming hug, a listening ear, and a respite from winter's winds. Simply put, you'll find room for *you*. Because I'm learning that the true definition of hospitality is simply making room.

This Christmas, let's make room.

Lord Jesus, teach me to make room for the
people in my life, just as You have made
room for me in Your kingdom. Amen.

Remember

Hospitality is far less about perfection and far more about simply making room.

RECLAIMING CHRISTMAS

Hospitality doesn't have to be hard. Don't worry about place settings and fine china; paper plates are fine. Potlucks or pizzas make quick work of dinner. And a fresh batch of slice-and-bake cookies not only provides a dessert everyone loves but also makes a home smell deliciously warm and welcoming. Yes, there may be one of those white-gloved, quick-to-judge, inspector types among your guests. Let their sniffs and comments melt away like Christmas snow. Welcome others into your heart and home simply because the Savior welcomes you into His.

Everything Changed

Now there were in the same country
shepherds living out in the fields, keeping
watch over their flock by night.

LUKE 2:8, NKJV

It was just another night out in the fields. The fire crackled, the shepherds wandered sleepily among their flocks, a lamb called softly for its mother and was softly answered in return. Just another night, like so many others before it, until . . . the skies filled with light and song and angels.

The shepherds listened in awed astonishment to the good news that would bring great joy to all people. They soaked up and savored the angel's words of a Savior born in Bethlehem, and then they ran to find Him.

It was just another night out in the fields, but it was a night that changed everything.

Everything.

Have we allowed that long-ago, faraway night to change everything for us? Does the good news fill us with awed astonishment? Has the miracle of that moment sent us running to the manger? Or are we still back among the sheep?

Today may seem like just another day, but it's not. Not really. Today is the day God is calling you to the Savior, just as He does every day. Run to Jesus, and let Him change everything for you.

*Lord my Shepherd, change
me—change every part of me—
to be more like You. Amen.*

Remember

Jesus came to
change everything.

RECLAIMING CHRISTMAS

Tonight, when all the house is tucked away and sleeping, turn off all the lights except those on the tree. Lie down under its branches—shove away a package or two if you need to—and gaze up into the lights. Yes, I know it sounds a bit silly, but it's a different perspective that allows us to consider a different point of view. Spend some time simply thinking about those long-ago, faraway shepherds, the wonders they witnessed, and how everything changed, both for them and for you. Tomorrow night, bring your flock.

DAY

15

The Perfect Home

Christ will make his home in your
hearts as you trust in him.

EPHESIANS 3:17, NLT

I'm quite sure a stable was not what Mary had in mind for her new-born child. But it was what God had in mind. That humble abode for the animals was His definition of a perfect first "home" for His Son.

Maybe Mary noticed the dust motes floating up from the hay. Perhaps she saw that the wooden beams were rough and splintered with use and didn't match the floor. Maybe she thought a few more candles and a wreath on the door would be just the thing to make the place a bit more festive. But probably not. I think Mary was wholly captivated by the ones with her in that little home rather than by how perfect—or imperfect—it appeared.

Could we do the same? Could we let go of the pressures of keeping up appearances and allow ourselves to be wholly captivated by the ones we love? What if we didn't put up three Pinterest-worthy trees with color-coordinated trim? What if we didn't cover the roof with strings of lights? Let's not get so caught up in creating the perfect holiday home that we forget to create *His* perfect home—a home filled with love.

Lord, remind me that it is not the outward
appearance but the heart of my home
that matters most to You. Amen.

Remember

The perfect home is
the home filled with
Christ and His love.

RECLAIMING CHRISTMAS

Decorating for Christmas can be overwhelming—trees, lights, garlands, wreaths, centerpieces, that hideous slightly cross-eyed Santa your great-aunt gave you. This year, decorate with only those things that bring joy to you and your loved ones. Ask each person in your family which decorations mean the most to them and put those out. If it's the Pinterest-perfect tree in every room, go for it. If it's the slightly misshapen Popsicle-stick star, that's beautiful too! And if it's the cross-eyed Santa . . . well, you do you. Decorate with the things that make you smile. Everything else is optional.

DAY

16

Savor
–the–
Sweetness

Mary gave birth to Jesus,
who is called the Messiah.

MATTHEW 1:16, NLT

Perhaps it's the mama in me, but I am endlessly fascinated by the image of Mary cradling the baby Jesus in her arms. Smiling in wonder as little fingers grasp her own. Counting ten impossibly tiny toes. Reaching to caress His cheek, marveling at the eyelashes fluttering against them as He sleeps, and wondering if this One so fresh from heaven dreams of the angels.

You can see Mary there, can't you? Eyes shining and so utterly caught up in the bundled Babe she can scarcely breathe in the holiness of the moment.

Because though we may not have held the Son of God in our arms, as mamas we have surely held those little ones made in His image. And in that sweet, holy stillness, we can still glimpse the face of God.

The stillness doesn't last long. Little ones grow with lightning speed, and quiet moments are quickly replaced with laughing, crawling, running, driving, not-so-little-anymore children who still manage to steal our breath away.

Today, forget about all those lists you haven't checked twice. Savor these sweet, holy moments . . . and smile.

*Holy and Most Precious Lord, fill me with
the wonder of my children and of that
Little One in Mary's arms. Amen.*

Remember

Savor the sweet,
holy moments of
motherhood.

RECLAIMING CHRISTMAS

Here's your task for today: savor the sweetness of your own littles—no matter how little or big they may be. Slip in while they're sleeping. Sit on the edge of the bed. Count fingers and toes. Stroke soft, sweet cheeks. Smooth tousled hair. Watch as they dream. And remember the Little One that Mary held so long ago. The Savior who came to earth to be like them, so that one day they could go to heaven and be with Him.

DAY

17

Learning
—to—
Lean

Because Mary's husband,
Joseph, was a good man . . .

MATTHEW 1:19, NCV

If the Bible's words were the script for a play, Joseph would have no lines to memorize, only assigned marks to hit upon the stage. Yet his role in the salvation story is essential. For God not only entrusted His Son to Mary, He entrusted both mother and Messiah to Joseph as well.

God knew Mary would need someone to lean on. And He knows you do too.

I know you, Mama. You're out there trying to be everything to everyone—and doing a pretty awesome job of it. But you weren't created to do it all or to be it all, all on your own.

Who is your Joseph? Maybe it's that "good man" who helps you weather the chaos, storms, and everyday minutiae of life. Or maybe it's someone else—family or friend. Or maybe you feel as if you're walking through this Christmas season alone, with no one to lean on. Let me offer this reminder: you are never alone. The One who came to be with His people is with you still. Learn to lean on the Savior. He won't let you fall.

God my Savior, when the chaos swirls
around me, remind me of the beautiful truth
that I can always lean on You. Amen.

Remember

Learn to lean on
the One who won't
let you fall.

RECLAIMING CHRISTMAS

When it comes to those classroom parties—whether it's school or church or whatever—there are a couple of things you should know. First, *don't try to do it all yourself*. Lean on your fellow moms and dads. Seriously, we're all in this together, and it doesn't have to be a five-star event. And second, *be careful what you become known for*. Because you will make it for every party until your child graduates and possibly beyond. Don't worry about impressing the other moms. Choose something that's sustainable when you've got a kid or two more—and an hour or two less—under your belt. Me? I'm the sausage-ball mom. *Rookie. Mistake.* Delicious, but *so* time-consuming! Learn from me. Be the napkin mom, the orange juice mom, the cupcakes-from-the-bakery mom. Don't be rookie-mistake mom.

Treasure

Mary treasured up all
these things and pondered
them in her heart.

LUKE 2:19

Today's verse is one of my favorites in the story of Jesus's birth. Yes, I love the whole story, the wonder of a God who would willingly choose to leave heaven and become a helpless babe to rescue the ones He loves. But this verse about Mary is special to me. As a mother, I relate to this treasuring and pondering of things.

By this point in her young life, Mary had already collected such incredible treasures to ponder and store in her heart: a conversation with an angel, the miracle of Elizabeth's baby, the shepherds rushing in with angelic news, and that Little One whose bright eyes watched her from the manger where He lay.

In my mind's eye, I see Mary in that stable, quietly savoring these moments, lost in the wonder. And I long to join her, if only for a minute. Don't you? So why don't we? Pause and put aside the list of things to be done. Step away from the laptop and phone. Forget the mess waiting to be cleaned. Instead, gather the nearest child into your arms. Close your eyes and ponder. Breathe in the holiness of the moment. And treasure the truth of God come down.

Fill my heart, O Lord,
with the joy and awe and
wonder of You. Amen.

Remember

God came

down . . . for you.

RECLAIMING CHRISTMAS

One day, our littles will not be so little anymore. They'll move out, make homes, and put up trees of their own. Give them tangible memories to treasure and take with them. Every year, let each child pick out an ornament. Yes, let *them* choose. It's a reflection of who they are in that moment. (Which explains the ballerina bear, assortment of soccer balls and basketballs, and the Santa-hat-wearing alligator playing the sax—no lie—that adorn my own tree.) If possible, inscribe the child's name and date on the bottom or back. Not only will your children have a collection of ornaments to take to their own homes but you'll have a collection of sweet and story-filled memories to unwrap and ponder each year until then.

DAY

19

Be Amazed

The child's father and mother
marveled at what was said about him.

LUKE 2:33

When the time was right, Mary and Joseph carried the baby Jesus to the temple to present Him to the Lord and so fulfill the law. Simeon—who had been promised that his eyes would see the Messiah before death saw him—did indeed see his Savior there. And he praised God for the bundle of salvation he held in his own arms.

But look at the words following those praises: "The child's father and mother marveled at what was said about him."

I can't help but wonder at their wonder. Had they not both been visited by angels and by shepherds seeking the Savior? Why did they marvel? How could they marvel? Perhaps it was forty days of life with a newborn. Forty days of dirty diapers and midnight feedings. Forty days of God being fully human that caused some of the extraordinary to become *ordinary*.

In our homes, we are surrounded by little ones—and not-so-little ones—all created in the image of the Divine, yet oh so fully and completely human. It's easy to allow the details and drudgery of daily life to steal away the wonder of them. Today, allow yourself to be amazed by the ordinary.

Lord, it's so easy to lose sight of all the
extraordinary You have poured into my
life. Open my eyes to see. Amen.

Remember

Make time to marvel
in the wonders of
the ordinary.

RECLAIMING CHRISTMAS

Sometimes, in order to see the extraordinary, we need to break out of the ordinary. Change things up a bit, and be a child again. Forget some of those chores today, and build a fort instead. You remember how, don't you? Pull the sheets over the couch, the table, the backs of chairs. Weigh down edges with stacks of books. Toss in pillows. String up twinkle lights. (You're the adult now—you can do things like that!) Load up a tray with cookies and cocoa and crawl in there, Mama. Read, giggle, snuggle, play a game, or take a nap. Enjoy the extraordinary.

The Prince
–of–
Peace

For to us a child is born, to us a son is given,
and the government will be on his shoulders.
And he will be called Wonderful Counselor,
Mighty God, Everlasting Father, Prince of Peace.

ISAIAH 9:6

There are times when the thing about heaven that appeals to me most is its promised peace. The longing and searching for that sweet relief is both universal and timeless. So is the answer. Peace is found in the Prince of Peace.

When I think of the shepherds kneeling at the manger, of Simeon and Anna cradling the infant Christ in their arms and, later, of the wise men bowing before the Son of God, I am envious. Imagine what they must have felt, knowing that they were seeing, touching, and holding the answer to all humanity's prayers. What peace there must have been in His presence. What peace there is in His presence still.

I said this would not be a book of "Thou shalts," but, really, there is one thing we *must* do if we want to find peace and calm in the midst of our Christmas storms. What is it that is burdening you during this holiday season? *Go to Jesus.* Lay down the heavy load at His feet in prayer—and leave it in His care. Seek the strength, solace, and shield of His Word, even if only a verse or two. Slip away with the Savior, and rest in His peace.

Sweet Prince of Peace, I lay all my burdens,
worries, and endless tasks at Your feet.
Please fill me with Your rest. Amen.

Remember

Let Jesus be your calm in the Christmas storms.

RECLAIMING CHRISTMAS

Slip away with Jesus. Such a beautiful thought for a busy mom, yet so very difficult to actually do. Of course, there's the old advice about rising early or staying up late . . . but, oh, sleep . . . sweet, precious sleep. Here's what I have found to be helpful: Seize the snatches of time that pop up in the day. Be ready to pray. Be armed with a Bible or an app on your phone. Whether it's in the shower (my secret hiding place—*shhh!*), waiting in a line, or in a moment of midnight stillness, seize the time and slip away with the Savior.

The Unexpected

When [Herod] had called together all the
people's chief priests and teachers of the law,
he asked them where the Messiah was to be
born. "In Bethlehem in Judea," they replied.

MATTHEW 2:4–5

Mary never expected to be the mother of the Messiah. Joseph never expected to marry an already pregnant wife. And the shepherds never expected the skies to fill with angels or to hear the heavenly harmony of the world's first hallelujah chorus.

Mary, Joseph, and those long-ago shepherds chose to embrace the unexpected, and their lives were forever changed.

But when Herod summoned the priests and the teachers of the law, when they read the prophecy, and when they quoted it to the king, those priests and teachers chose to ignore the unexpected. They didn't follow the wise men or even send along a spy. They didn't search out the baby who just might have been—who, in fact, was—the Messiah they claimed to be waiting for. They chose not to embrace the unexpected, and their lives, too, were forever changed.

When the unexpected comes our way this Christmas season—and it will—let's choose to embrace it. To live and laugh and love right in the midst of it. Because if we don't, we just might miss the greatest gifts of all.

When the unexpected comes my way,
Lord, show me the beauty and blessings
hidden within it. Amen.

Remember

Learn to live, laugh, and love in the unexpected moments of life.

RECLAIMING CHRISTMAS

Christmas with kids is an invitation for the unexpected. Unexpected giggles, unexpected tears, and most definitely unexpected messes. Messes in the kitchen, in the playroom, on their hands, and all over their sweet, sticky faces. Don't stress and rush to put it "right." Meet them in the middle of the mess—with a smile, with grace, with a willingness to make a mess of your own. Let them help bake the cookies, paint the ornaments, and decorate the tree. I've learned the moments and memories are more important than the mess. Oh, also, a box of wipes is your best friend.

DAY

22

The Perfect Gift

On coming to the house, they saw the child with his mother Mary, and they bowed down and worshiped him. Then they opened their treasures and presented him with gifts of gold, frankincense and myrrh.

MATTHEW 2:11

When the three wise men followed that shining star all the way to Bethlehem and to Jesus, they came bearing gifts. Gold for the King. Frankincense for the worship of God. And myrrh for the Savior who would one day be sacrificed. Their choices were no doubt divinely guided by the God who knew the young family would soon need the riches as they fled Herod's coming wrath. The wise men's gifts were more than perfect; they were providential.

Do you ever find yourself on a quest for the perfect gift? The gift that is met by joyful shrieks of laughter, jump-in-your-arms hugs, and bright, happy smiles? Perhaps it's the teddy bear that quickly becomes a constant companion. The jersey that's instantly tugged on. Or the book that can't be put down until the last page is turned. Giving truly is the greater joy, especially when we find that perfect gift.

There's an even more perfect gift we can give our loved ones, though. It's the gift of ourselves, of our presence in the moment. We so easily get tangled up in thoughts of what comes next and what's needed next that we miss the moment. Still your spinning thoughts and simply be present. It's the perfect gift.

Immanuel, You are present here with me. Amid all the rush and hurry of this season, remind me to pause and be fully present with the ones I love. Amen.

Remember

Pause and
be present.

MERRY
CHRISTMAS

RECLAIMING CHRISTMAS

Sometimes the best gifts are also the simplest. They're the ones
that light the spark of creativity and unleash our joy. They can
even be as simple as a cardboard box. (And with online shopping,
don't we all have more than a few?) Give your littles a giant
box or a bunch of smaller ones. Add a fistful of crayons and
markers—and permission to let their imaginations run wild. What
will they make? A puppet show stage or a playhouse? Maybe a
castle, a bobsled, or even a time machine? Don't forget to grab
some of those crayons yourself and join in the fun. Because it's
your time and presence that will make this the perfect present.

DAY

23

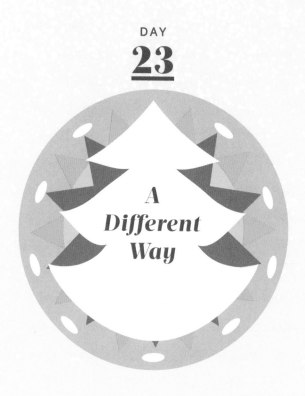

A
Different
Way

God warned the wise men in a dream not
to go back to Herod, so they returned to
their own country by a different way.

MATTHEW 2:12, NCV

The time had come for the wise men to return home. They had searched for the new King, and they had found Him in Bethlehem. But old King Herod did not share their delight in this threat to his throne. Even if that threat was still toddling at his mother's side. Even if that threat was the Son of God Most High.

Though Herod was eager to hear the wise men's report, God would not allow it. The wise men were warned, and they traveled home by a different way.

There's great wisdom in the men's actions. Because sometimes confrontation is counterproductive. And sometimes—oftentimes—it's better to simply travel by a different way. God's Word says it this way: "Do your best to live in peace with everyone" (Romans 12:18, NCV). Or, as I tell my own littles, smile and just keep walking.

Because there's always a Herod. Always that person—a relative, a friend, a foe, a neighbor, a random Jane or Joe in the miles-long checkout line—who's looking to make trouble. Smile and just keep walking. Travel by a different way.

Lord, please give me the wisdom to
know when I should speak and when I
should just keep walking. Amen.

Remember

Sometimes we simply need to smile and travel by a different way.

RECLAIMING CHRISTMAS

When you're traveling—by the main way or a different way—you often need a quick and easy gift to take along. This edible treat is both salty and sweet, as well as deliciously satisfying. Top a small pretzel with a chocolate-covered caramel (like a Rolo). Repeat with as many pretzels and caramels as you'd like. Bake on a parchment-lined cookie sheet at 325° for 3 minutes. Remove from the oven and immediately push a peanut M&M into the caramel. Allow to cool, then place in a pretty tin for gifting. Or keep them for yourself. There's no judgment here.

Such Good News

Suddenly, the angel was joined by a vast host of others—the armies of heaven—praising God and saying, "Glory to God in highest heaven, and peace on earth to those with whom God is pleased."

LUKE 2:13–14, NLT

The holidays are filled with "day befores." The day before the party. The day before the play. And, of course, the day before Christmas. And while we don't know the exact date of Jesus's birth, we do know that there *was* a day before that first Christmas. Can you imagine that day, in that long-ago time and faraway place?

Mary and Joseph are likely nearing the outskirts of a busy and bustling Bethlehem. The innkeeper is tending his inn full of guests. And nearby the shepherds are quietly counting their sheep. It is an unsuspecting world.

But in the hallways of heaven, on that day before, the angels are preparing. The host hums, practicing their song. *Tomorrow* is the day they've been waiting so long to see and to sing about. *Tomorrow* they will fly to the fields to share with shepherds the good news of the Savior being born.

Their tomorrow is our today. Because Christ was born. And all the promises of salvation made by God the Father are kept in God the Son.

Imagine that day. Practice your songs. And praise God for the good news.

Lord, my Father, as I think about that long-ago night,
I am utterly amazed at Your willingness to send Your
Son to this earth—and I am so very grateful. Amen.

Remember

Sing songs of praise
to Christ the King.

RECLAIMING CHRISTMAS

On this night—no matter what the calendar shows it to be—join with heaven's angels and lift up your voice in song. Don't worry if you're slightly off-key or the beat isn't quite right. Teach your children the words—yes, to the silly, fun songs, but to the classic ones too. Sing of the silent night and that long-ago first noel. Let your voices carry you to the little town of Bethlehem and to the Babe sleeping far away in the manger. Practice your praises with your loved ones tonight.

DAY

25

**Because
Jesus
Was Born**

His kingdom will never end.

LUKE 1:33

I think about the world Jesus was born into—a world of foreign occupation and murderous kings. Of lying officials and cheating tax collectors. A world that, in many ways, is not so very different from our own.

Solomon once declared, "There is nothing new under the sun" (Ecclesiastes 1:9). And when it comes to the chaos, evil, and sin of mankind, his words prove to be far truer than we would like them to be. Especially when we look into the eyes of the little ones looking to us to show them the way. Yet this worldly kingdom—this world we and ours were born into—is only temporary. It's the kingdom of Christ that will last forever.

While we don't know all the details about the heaven that is coming, we know this beautiful truth: "God will wipe away every tear from their eyes; there shall be no more death, nor sorrow, nor crying. There shall be no more pain" (Revelation 21:4, NKJV). Our souls long for heaven, our home.

And someday we will be there, in that Kingdom that never ends. All because Jesus was born into this world.

Lord, My Redeemer, I praise You for this
life You've given me—and for the promise
of life forever with You. Amen.

Remember

Because Jesus was
born, heaven is
waiting for you.

RECLAIMING CHRISTMAS

Gather your Bible, your littles, not-so-littles, and bigs. Let them
climb onto your lap, lean over your shoulder, and hear the words
of God from your own lips. There is power in that, Mama. Don't
neglect it. Feed and fuel it. Skip the storybook Bible this time, and
read from your own. Let them see how much the Word matters
to you. Let them watch your fingers turn the pages and trace the
text. Let them hear the words of God, the story of the Savior
from your own heart. Imprint this memory on their hearts, minds,
and souls. This memory of Mama sharing the Good News.

DAY

26

God
—with—
Us

"Behold, the virgin shall be with child, and
bear a Son, and they shall call His name
Immanuel," which is translated, "God with us."

MATTHEW 1:23, NKJV

In the Garden of Eden, Adam and Eve strolled with God in the cool of the day. Abraham spoke to Him as a friend. Moses met with God in the flames of a bush, in a pillar of cloud, and high atop a mountain. In those days, it took something of a miracle to be with God.

But when Jesus came—when He was laid in that manger, when His chubby toddler feet took those first tentative steps in the dust of this world—the relationship changed. The Lord came to live among His people. He looked into their eyes. Listened to their voices. And touched them with His own hands. He was truly Immanuel. *God with us.*

And when the tomb was found empty, when the Savior had done all He came to do, everything changed again.

We don't need a garden, a cloud, a mountain, or a miracle to meet with our Lord. Because God was not content to live beside us or among us, He came to live within us. He's as close as your next heartbeat.

*God of All Grace, still my thoughts
and fill me with the knowledge of Your
Spirit living within me. Amen.*

Remember

God was not content
to simply be near us,
so He came to
live within us.

RECLAIMING CHRISTMAS

Christmas is the celebration of God's greatest gift, and so it has become a time for giving gifts. As a mom, you've likely gotten lots of them. Sweet pictures framed in Popsicle sticks, thumbprint angels with crooked wings, and oh-so carefully crafted yet weirdly shaped and unrecognizable hunks of clay that, upon careful investigation, turn out to be fish. What's a mom to do with all these gifts? Cherish them. Place them proudly on the shelf for all the world to see. And tell anyone who asks about the little hands that made them.

*Escape
–and–
Be Still*

An angel of the Lord appeared to Joseph in
a dream. "Get up," he said, "take the child
and his mother and escape to Egypt."

MATTHEW 2:13

The wise men had barely reached the edge of Bethlehem on their journey home when an angel appeared to Joseph in a dream. He warned of a jealous, mad king with murder on his mind and urged an escape to Egypt. No stranger to heavenly visitors, Joseph quickly rose, gathered Mary and the now-toddling Jesus, and escaped into the night.

Escaped into the night. While I have no desire to be forced to flee for my life, I'll confess that the thought of escape sometimes sounds quite alluring. Do you ever long to escape? For a few hours, a minute, a moment to breathe? Surely, I'm not the only one.

Because even after Christmas has passed, and it's time to undo much of what I've spent the last few weeks doing, I find myself wanting to simply be still. To escape. It feels like such a luxury, but is it? Or might it be the very thing we need most?

King David, a man after God's heart, once heard God's voice commanding him to "Be still, and know that I am God" (Psalm 46:10). And don't we all need that reminder sometimes? *God is God.* Not us and not our schedules, but God. Heed that still, small voice that whispers into the weariness. For a minute or a moment, escape and *be still* with God.

Father of Peace, when this world overwhelms
me, remind me to pause, be still, and
escape into Your presence. Amen.

Remember

Be still and know
that God is God.

RECLAIMING CHRISTMAS

Escape can be as simple as something warm and chocolaty in a favorite mug. For a decadent, homemade cocoa mix, stir together 3 cups of instant nonfat dry milk, ⅔ cup of sugar, and ¾ cup of baking cocoa. Store in a large glass jar. (Hiding this jar is optional, but highly recommended.) To serve, add a half-cup of the mix to your favorite mug, and stir in a cup of hot water. Embellish with marshmallows, a peppermint stick, dark chocolate chips, a splash of coffee, or a sprinkle of sea salt—whatever your heart desires. And . . . *escape*. Oh, and just like those slice-and-bake cookies, pre-packaged cocoa counts!

It's Personal

For God so loved the world that he gave his
one and only Son, that whoever believes in
him shall not perish but have eternal life.

JOHN 3:16

John 3:16 is one of the pivotal verses of the Bible. Let's make it personal, shall we? Because it is so very personal—to God, to Jesus, to you and me.

Jesus left heaven to come to earth. Think about that for a moment. He *willingly* stepped away from the peace and perfection of heaven to come to this earth. To be born as a helpless baby. To grow up through the stumbles of childhood and all the awkwardness and angst of adolescence. To become fully human. To work and laugh, hurt and cry. To experience the same joys, trials, temptations, and struggles that we do. And then, to die. For us.

Over two thousand years ago, Jesus left heaven to meet us in the midst of all we are and to offer us the hope of all He created us to be. He does it still today. He joins us in the deadlines and piles of laundry, as we scrub sticky fingers and faces, and as we wait for teens to pull into the drive. Christ comes to each of us *personally*.

*My Lord, Immanuel, I cannot fathom the
kind of love that would send You from
heaven to be by my side. But I claim it, I
cling to it, and I praise You for it. Amen.*

Remember

Jesus meets you where you are, to help you become all He created you to be.

RECLAIMING CHRISTMAS

Jesus died to give us life in Him (John 10:10). A life that is "rich and satisfying" (NLT), "in abundance . . . to the full, till it overflows" (AMPC). Are we living that life? Or are we lost in the dust and dirt, the deadlines and distractions? Do something today that fills you up, that makes you feel alive and overflowing. Maybe it's as simple as blowing bubbles with a child (or without), taking a walk, or laughing until your sides hurt. Or maybe it's something more, like surprising a neighbor with an unexpected gift, volunteering at a shelter, or helping where your heart sees a need. Live abundantly today.

DAY

29

Who
–Are–
You?

When the right time came, God sent his Son, born
of a woman, subject to the law. God sent him to
buy freedom for us who were slaves to the law, so
that he could adopt us as his very own children.

GALATIANS 4:4–5, NLT

Do you know who you are? I don't mean your name, your job title, or your wife-mama-sister-daughter role in life. I mean, do you know who you are in the eyes of the One who created you? Because when push comes to shove, His is the only opinion that eternally matters.

Every person on this planet is fearfully and wonderfully made in the image of the Creator. Yes, including you. God's love for us is unending, unlimited, and unfailing in ways we can only begin to imagine. He has good plans—kingdom plans—for you and me, for each and every one of us. And when we choose to step into those plans by believing, by loving, and by following His Son, the Lord steps into our lives in the boldest of ways. By His unfathomable mercy and grace, we are transformed from creations of God into children of God.

As this year winds to a close and the new one is peering over the horizon, take with you into the future this precious, life-changing answer to the question of who you are: *You* are the one God sent His Son to save. *You* are a daughter of the King.

Lord, in the crush and clutter of the day, it's
so easy to forget who I really am. Help me
remember that I am Your beloved child. Amen.

Remember

Of all the names and
titles you wear, the
greatest is daughter
of the King.

RECLAIMING CHRISTMAS

God's grace isn't just for others, you know. It isn't just for the mama with the perfectly put-together house who serves gourmet meals that even the pickiest child raves about. His mercy isn't just for the never-a-hair-out-of-place mama whose child wouldn't dream of misbehaving at story hour. His love—His lavish love—is for *you*. *You* have a place at His table. *Your* voice is heard. *You* are an heir in His kingdom. Your challenge today? Simply to hang out with these truths. As you go about the tasks of the day, meditate on them. Soak them in. Believe you are who He says you are.

DAY

<u>30</u>

Returning Home

When Jesus' parents had fulfilled all the
requirements of the law of the Lord, they
returned home to Nazareth in Galilee.

LUKE 2:39, NLT

What a season it had been for Joseph and Mary. A long journey to Bethlehem, no room at the inn, angels, shepherds, and the Son of God come down to nap in their arms. In many ways, it must have been both a relief and a comfort to return to the rhythms and routines of home.

While our journey through the holidays is nothing compared to all that Joseph and Mary experienced, the post-holiday season does feel a bit like returning home after it's all over—even if we never really left. We return home to a house made more spacious and airy by the taking down of all the holiday trappings of garlands, ornaments, and bows. We settle back into the familiar, comfortable, and predictable rhythms of everyday life.

As the year comes to a close, it's time for wrapping up and winding down. But before you pack it all away, before you settle back into those routines, take a moment to pause and to reflect.

Has this been the holiday you wanted it to be? Have you found Christ in this Christmas? Has there been time to share with your family the wonders of kneeling at the manger? Or are there things you want to revise and change so that next year it will be simply Christmas?

Lord Jesus, wherever the days and the seasons take me, I know I am always home when I am with You. Amen.

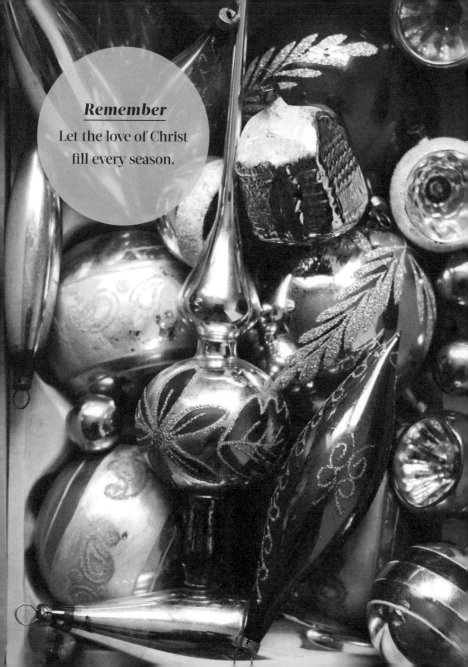

Remember

Let the love of Christ
fill every season.

RECLAIMING CHRISTMAS

As I pack all things Christmas away for next year, it's so tempting to rush and just "get it done." But I've learned that a bit of mindful packing now will save me so much time and so many headaches next year. I give each room its own box (or boxes). A quickly added label describes the box's contents—kitchen, bonus room lights, mantel decor. Then, when Christmas rolls around again, it's simple to pull out just the right box to decorate one room at a time, minimizing the chaos. And if the box containing that hideous, slightly cross-eyed Santa just happens to get shoved aside and forgotten . . . well, moms do what moms gotta do.

A
New
Way

You have made known to me the
paths of life; you will fill me
with joy in your presence.

ACTS 2:28

The New Year is coming. Don't let it pass by in a blur of life, untouched and unchanged by the holiness of the season.

I'm not saying we should rush to make a list of resolutions for all the things we will and won't do in the coming year. I confess I've made and abandoned far too many of those resolutions for that process to inspire me. This year, why don't we try something different? Instead of launching into a litany of lists, let's take this time to begin settling into a new way of living and thinking by allowing the God who is with us to truly be *with us*.

Because Christ isn't only for Christmas.

These lessons we've learned kneeling at the manger are not lessons to tuck away until next December rolls around. They're the truths that will carry us through all the days and seasons of the year to come, and they're the truths that will give meaning, purpose, and joy to our lives.

Continue on these holy pathways Christ has carved into your heart this season. They'll lead you to the things that matter—moments with family, laughter with friends, and drawing ever closer to Him.

Lord, lead me along the pathways
that You have carved out for me.
Lead me ever closer to You. Amen.

Remember

Christ is so
much more than
Christmas.

RECLAIMING CHRISTMAS

⬥

This coming new year stretches out before us like an empty page, and the hand of God is poised over it, ready to write. The question is this: *Will we let Him?* Will we allow that blessing into our lives? Or will we snatch away the pen and hurriedly scribble through the days as we rush from one must-do to the next. Put down the pen, sweet friend. Close your eyes—just for a moment. Breathe deeply of His presence. Now, open your eyes to the wonder of Christ all around you. Repeat often and as needed, every day.

Simply Christmas